STUDENT BOOK

WORRY WORRY WORRY

School, War and Other Scary Stuff

An involving 13-session course to
help high school students grapple
with fears and worries

By Katie Abercrombie

Group
Books
Loveland, Colorado

Worry, Worry, Worry: School, War and Other Scary Stuff Student Book

Copyright © 1988 by Katie Abercrombie
First Printing

Credits
Edited by Nancy M. Shaw
Designed by Judy Atwood
Illustrations by RoseAnne Buerge

Scripture quotations are from the Holy Bible, New International Version. Copyright © 1973, 1978, 1984 International Bible Society. Used by permission of Zondervan Bible Publishers.

ISBN 0931-529-49-2

Printed in the United States of America

Contents

Section One:

Fear and Worries—How Do We Handle Them?

What? Me Afraid?

F ear. Worry. Anxiety. These feelings are part of daily life. There are many things to be afraid of—not measuring up, losing a friend or family member, not having control over one's life. These fears and worries surface in many different ways in teenagers' lives— being afraid to try out for the team, feeling distraught when a friend seems angry, worrying about a facial blemish, feeling anxious about world events. Sometimes fear is obvious; sometimes it's hidden. What is certain is that fear is a common experience.

Objectives

In this session you will:

• become acquainted with the course and the other participants.

• discover differences between fear, anxiety, worry and panic.

• discuss obvious and hidden worries.

• explore fearful feelings Mary might have had as Jesus' mother.

• begin to understand the roots of your fears.

• start to think about God's role in dealing with fears.

Fearful People Bingo

Instructions: Examine the worksheet. Find someone with a particular fear or worry and ask that person to sign in the appropriate space.

Find someone who . . .

is afraid of the dark.	panics when confronted with a snake.	worries about his or her looks.	feels anxious before a big test.	worries about losing a parent.
is afraid of fire.	procrastinates planning for the future.	jumps when someone says, "Boo!"	is nervous at the dentist.	worries about losing friends.
is anxious about trying any new skill.	feels he or she must always be perfectly groomed.	has been afraid to tell about something he or she did wrong.	won't watch scary movies.	worries about nuclear war.
always locks his or her car doors.	would be anxious if a stranger started a conversation with him or her.	feels pressured to achieve.	has been afraid of getting beat up.	has worried himself or herself sick.
has let fear of failure stop him or her from trying something new.	would panic if someone suddenly pointed a gun at him or her.	worries about his or her grades.	gets butterflies before speaking in front of a group.	gets sick at the sight of blood.

Mary's Diary

Instructions: Listen to the following introduction, then read the assigned scripture passages. Think about how Mary must have felt in that situation. Write what she might have written in her diary. Focus on the fears she might have had.

Mary, Jesus' mother, was a young woman, perhaps a teenager, when the angel told her she was pregnant. She was an unmarried virgin, engaged to Joseph. Think about the fears she must have experienced. What would her family think? What would Joseph do? Even in the months and years that followed, she must have experienced many fearful times.

Mary's fears and worries

Matthew 1:18-25	Luke 2:6-7
Luke 1:26-38	Luke 2:8-20
Luke 1:39-56	Matthew 2:1-18
Luke 2:1-5	Luke 2:41-52

A page from Mary's diary . . .

Dear Diary,
I'm so frightened. I'm not sure I understand.

Anxiety ... Worry ... Fear ... Panic!

Instructions: The following words will be used throughout this course. Listen to your leader's instructions on what to do with the information you find on this page.

There are many words we use to describe fear—uneasiness, insecurity, apprehension, alarm, terror—but the following words will be used frequently during this course. Here is how we will define them:

Anxiety—A response to an anticipated danger; a concern about what might happen.

Worry—An expression of nervous energy; a way people express fear or anxiety; what they do when they are anxious or afraid.

Fear—Concern for one's personal safety; a response to a real, physical threat.

Panic—A sudden, overwhelming terror, possibly interfering with or prompting constructive action.

Roots of fear

The specific things we are afraid of may vary, but most fears are usually rooted in one of the following fears:

Fear of loss of life or personal injury. Examples include fear of heights, firearms, snakes, speeding cars, contaminated food or crime.

Fear of loss of love. Examples include fear of parents' fighting, losing a loved one via death or divorce, or offending someone so he or she cuts off or ends a relationship.

Fear of loss of self-esteem. Examples include fear of speaking in public, making a mistake, looking less than perfect or trying something new.

Fear of loss of control. Examples include fear about global issues such as nuclear war and worldwide poverty or overconcern with rules and details.

Think about your own fears

What are some of your fears in the area of . . .

loss of life or personal injury?

loss of self-esteem?

loss of love?

loss of control?

Why Faith Doesn't Take My Fears Away

S hould a Christian be afraid? Should Christians worry? It's easy to think that as Christians our fears and worries are behind us. Yet we do feel afraid and we do worry. Ministers get nervous before a sermon. Christian singers get stage fright. Volunteers at a shelter for the homeless get scared when an overnight resident seems threatening. All of these people are Christians doing work to serve God, yet they experience fear. Christian teenagers also worry, feel anxious and are afraid. Why doesn't faith take our fears away?

Objectives

In this session you will:

• share how faith has helped you deal with fears and worries.

• look at how two people of the Bible handled their fears.

• learn about a present-day Christian who experienced fear.

• ask the question, "Does faith take my fears away?"

• read and listen to reassurances from the Bible.

Fearful People, Faithful People

Instructions: Read the introductory material and suggested scripture passages assigned to your group. Then read and answer the discussion questions.

Esther's story

Esther was a beautiful young Jewish woman who was chosen to replace the banished Vashti as queen to King Xerxes of Persia and Media. On the advice of her cousin Mordecai, Esther didn't tell anyone she was Jewish. The king's evil prime minister, Haman, became angry because Mordecai, whom he knew to be a Jew, refused to bow down to him. Haman schemed to persuade the king to sign a proclamation authorizing the slaughter of the Jewish people. But Mordecai asked Esther to intervene for the Jewish people.

Read Esther 3:1-11; 4:1-17; 5:1-8; 7:1-10.
Discuss these questions:

1. What did Mordecai ask Esther to do?

2. How did Esther respond at first?

3. Why was she afraid?

4. How did she handle her fear?

5. Where did she draw her strength from to act in spite of her fear?

continued

Peter's story

When Jesus was with the disciples, Peter did everything he could to identify with him. Even though he didn't understand why Jesus wanted to wash his feet, Peter encouraged him to wash his head and his hands as well. At their last meal together, Peter boldly proclaimed that he would die for Jesus. Yet later, as Jesus predicted, Peter denied even knowing Jesus.

But after Jesus' death, Resurrection and Ascension, Peter became a bold apostle for Christ. This stubborn, abrasive fisherman became a leader whose words and actions demonstrated his faith.

Read John 13:36-38; 18:15-18, 25-27; Acts 3:1-16; 4:1-14.

Discuss these questions:

1. What was Peter afraid of?

2. How did he handle his fear?

3. How was Peter different in the stories in Acts?

4. What gave Peter strength in spite of his fear for his safety?

After you've completed your Bible study, combine with the other groups who worked on the same study and develop a creative way to share your story with the other participants.

Joni's Story

Instructions: Read each section of the story and answer the questions that follow. Discuss your answers with the group.

Joni (pronounced "Johnny") Eareckson Tada, at age 17, was almost completely paralyzed from a diving accident. In a brief moment, her life was turned upside down. There would be no more swimming, riding or hiking; no more dating, going out with friends or just eating a normal meal with her family; no more combing her own hair, feeding herself or even tending to her bodily functions. She had made plans for college that fall and had been dating a special boy. Now she couldn't even use her arms and legs.

Discuss these questions:

1. Imagine yourself in Joni's situation. Your legs won't move and you have limited control of your upper arms. You can move your head and neck and you can speak, but you are dependent upon others' care. Close your eyes and think about how this physical change would alter your life. Brainstorm some of the fears and worries you think Joni might have had. Here are some ideas to get you started: "Who will take care of me?" "I'll be embarrassed when I try to eat." "What about the rest of my life—my career, my marriage?" "Will my friends still like me?" List other fears and worries Joni might have had.

2. Which of these fears would concern you most if you were in Joni's situation? Why?

Joni was a Christian. She had great faith that God wanted her to be healed. She prayed, and her friends and family prayed. Healing services were held, but she didn't improve. She went through a period of doubting God and his promises. She was afraid all that was left for her were hospitals, therapy and watching television. She was sickened at the thought of learning to use her body as it was. She began to lose hope. *continued*

3. Imagine how Joni must have felt when she realized God wasn't going to answer her prayers the way she wanted. Think about how you would have felt in the same situation. Would you have been depressed? hopeless? afraid? angry? List the feelings you'd have had in Joni's situation.

4. Do you think God will take our fears away or solve all our problems if we have enough faith? Why or why not?

Fortunately, Joni had Christian friends and family members who supported and loved her during this time. She had people who could listen to her fears and help her search the scriptures for words of hope and encouragement. She came out of her depression. She worked hard in therapy to become as independent as possible and learn new ways of coping with life. She learned to use a wheelchair. She became an accomplished artist by holding a pen in her mouth. She moved out of the hospital to live with her sister who cared for her with the help of friends. Joni's life was different from what it was, but she was content.

5. Imagine what it must have been like for Joni to realize she had to start over again. What sources of support did she use?

6. How would you have responded to this new start? What sources of support would you use? How would your faith affect your response to this type of situation?

A Window of Fear, Faith and Me

Instructions: Read the open-ended sentences in the windowpanes below. Complete the sentences, find a partner and share your answers.

1. A time I didn't do something because I was afraid was when . . .

2. A time I hesitated because I was afraid to do what I knew was right was when . . .

3. When I know I have to do something, but I'm afraid or nervous about it, I . . .

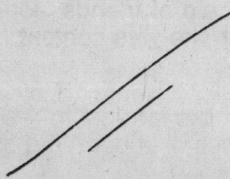

4. Lately, I've been worrying about . . .

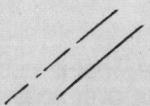

5. My Christian faith helps me deal with my fears and worries by . . .

6. When I'm fearful, anxious or worried, a Bible passage that reassures or strengthens me is . . . (Look in the Bible or a concordance to refresh your memory. The Psalms and Gospels offer numerous passages of support and reassurance. Copy the passage that means the most to you.)

Worrying Right

"**D**on't worry!" How many times have you heard that phrase? It's easy to say, but not so easy to do. Anxiety and worry are rampant in our society and are blamed for many of people's problems, including mental and emotional illness, stress, abuse and a never-ending list of physical ailments.

As bad as worry and anxiety can be for us, they also have their positive side. They let us know we have a problem that we need to do something about. They spur us to action and encourage us to make necessary changes. But worry and anxiety can paralyze us if we spend our time being worried instead of working on the problem.

Objectives

In this session you will:

• share some of your worries and the ways you cope with them.

• imagine some of the realistic and unrealistic worries a Bible character might have had.

• practice a problem-solving method on an imaginary situation.

• apply a problem-solving method to worries in your own life.

• affirm one another.

All Boxed In

Instructions: Using the box you were given, complete the following directions.

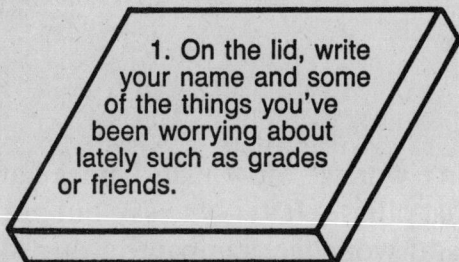

1. On the lid, write your name and some of the things you've been worrying about lately such as grades or friends.

2. On the four sides of your box, do the following:

Side 1—Draw pictures of what you usually do when you're worried such as biting your nails, pacing the floor or sleeping.

Side 2—List how your ways of worrying help or hurt you.

Side 3—Explain how you solved a recent worry.

Side 4—Write a worry you have now and why you think you haven't been able to solve it.

Worry, Worry

Instructions: Read Luke 7:36-50 and follow the directions.

1. Pretend you're the woman in this passage. List things she might have said to herself as she worried about going to the Pharisee's house to see Jesus.

2. Form a semicircle around one member of your group. Take turns reading the worries. Read them as if you were one of the woman's little voices telling her all the things that could go wrong. The group member who isn't reading should act out or mime these worries. For example, a person could bite his or her fingernails to mime "What will Jesus think of me?"

3. After everyone has read his or her worries, talk about the feelings everyone experienced. Which worries were most common? Which worries surprised you? With which worry did you identify most closely? Why?

GETTING OUT OF THE BOX

Instructions: Read the following problem-solving method. Ask questions to make sure you understand the process.

Worrying about a problem is rarely helpful. Worry boxes us in and keeps us from finding a solution. We can get out of the box and let worry help us, however, if we turn our worrying into problem-solving. Set up a time to work on what is worrying you. It won't help to worry about next week's history presentation while you're working on your math homework. Worrying about how you're going to explain your new job to your parents won't help while you listen to a friend who's trying to tell you about a problem. It's impossible to give your full attention to both what you are worried about and the situation at hand. When you can't give your problem your full attention, you may end up worrying all day without coming up with a solution. Set aside some time to work on your concern, using the following problem-solving steps:

1. *Define the problem.* Decide what situation is worrying you. Write it on paper as clearly as possible.

2. *Decide exactly what worries you about the situation.* If you're worried about a history presentation, ask yourself why. Are you afraid you won't be prepared? Are you afraid you might do something to embarrass yourself? Are you worried that the class might laugh at you or not pay attention to you? Are you afraid your hair or clothes won't look right? List all the things that worry you about the situation. Then write the worst possible thing that could happen.

continued

3. *Conduct a reality check.* Ask yourself what things are likely to happen. What things do you have control over? (These are the things you can do something about.) Dismiss concerns such as "I might trip while I'm walking to the front of the class" or "All they will think about is the zit on my nose." Fortunately, these things rarely happen.

Don't spend time worrying about the things you have no control over. You can't control whether your teacher will be in a good or bad mood, and there's no way you can determine who will do his or her presentation before you. Worrying about things you can't do anything about wastes your time and may make you more nervous.

4. *Choose the worries that you want to work on, and brainstorm ways to deal with them.* If you're concerned about not being prepared for the presentation, you might get some help from a friend, schedule time for more research and preparation, ask your teacher to clarify his or her expectations or go to the library to do some more reading. Ask a friend or a trusted adult for additional ideas. Pray about your concerns. Write your ideas on paper and think about how you can handle each concern.

5. *Choose solutions you think will best solve your problem, and make specific plans to implement them.* If you decide to ask your teacher to clarify his or her expectations, decide when and how you're going to do that. If you decide you need more time for research and preparation, decide how much time you'll need and write that time into your schedule.

6. *Get to work on your solutions and stop worrying.* You've made a good start on solving this problem!

Jennifer's Worries

Instructions: Read the problem and use the problem-solving method suggested in "Getting Out of the Box" for helping Jennifer solve her problem. Listen carefully to others' suggestions and reasoning as you work together.

Jennifer, a junior in high school, is assigned to do a project in her chemistry class with Kevin, one of the more popular boys in school. Jennifer is a good student but very shy. She doesn't know Kevin, but she does know he doesn't work hard on his studies. The project was assigned last week and is due in a month.

Neither Jennifer nor Kevin has said anything to the other about the project, or about anything else. Jennifer feels uncomfortable talking to popular boys. She's starting to feel nervous about the project, but she doesn't know what to do. Grades are important to her and her plans for college. She doesn't want to mess up this project, but she's also unsure about how to approach or work with Kevin.

6 Get to work on your solutions and stop worrying.

5 Choose solutions you think will best solve your problem, and make specific plans to implement them.

4 Choose the worries that you want to work on, and brainstorm ways to deal with them.

3 Conduct a reality check.

2 Decide exactly what worries you about the situation.

1 Define the problem.

Peace in the Storm

M any teenagers find they must deal with a serious life crisis during these difficult years. In some situations teenagers have little or no control. Parents die or get divorced. A family member becomes seriously ill or is injured. Alcohol or drug abuse creates a battleground in the home.

Other less serious situations can also cause anxiety. Friends move away. Cuts in pay force families to change their lifestyle. Schools establish rules that seem unfair.

World situations can add anxiety to teenagers' lives. An escalating arms race along with the proliferation of nuclear weapons can intensify worry. Continuing conflict between nations can develop a sense of hopelessness. Teenagers feel they can do little to control these problems. But they can learn how to control their response to these situations. They can learn how to control their worry and their concern.

Objectives

In this session you will:

• realize there are problems you can't change or control.

• discover ways to develop an attitude of hopefulness.

• discuss the importance of faith in order to experience "peace in the storm."

• think about God's role in the storms in your life.

• set personal goals for developing an attitude of hopefulness.

• express what "faith and peace in the storm" means to you by writing new words to "Amazing Grace."

Learning Station 1

"Looking on the 'Bright Side' "

"Look on the bright side!" How many times have you heard that advice? It doesn't seem to help much when storms are whipping around you and your world seems ready to collapse. Even in the midst of a real storm, with the clouds hiding the sun, the thunder crashing and the rain pouring down, you know that the sun is up there somewhere shining as brightly as always.

Life is like that for a Christian. You experience the storms of life, just like everyone else, but you know there is a promise of something better. Christ's love keeps shining, no matter what is happening in your life.

An important aspect of peace in the storm is a positive attitude, a hope that things will get better. With a positive attitude, you know that troubles and storms can help you grow as a person to develop your faith, compassion and strength. "Look on the bright side" may sound silly, but it helps you look at your problems with a more hopeful attitude.

Here are some examples of a hopeful, positive attitude during a storm:

Crisis	Hopeful attitude
1. My family has been transferred. I have to move away from all of my friends.	This isn't going to be an easy move, but it will give me a chance to start over again, to make new friends and perhaps to make some changes in my lifestyle.
2. My father was arrested for driving drunk. The court says he must go to therapy or go to jail. The court also says the family has to go to therapy with him!	Even though this experience has been a terrible strain on my family, I know that getting help may be the best thing for all of us.

continued

A positive attitude doesn't mean that your storms aren't important or that you don't hurt. Moving away from friends is scary, and a family crisis is hard to deal with. Losing a family member or going through a divorce also hurts. Allow yourself time to grieve and experience your emotions. A positive, hopeful attitude will help you look for the best in all situations and know that things will get better.

Read Romans 5:1-5 in your small group. Complete two of the following sentences. Choose one sentence and talk about it with your group.

1. To me, the most important word in this passage is _____ because _____
_____
_____

2. A time a storm in my life helped me grow was when
_____
_____
_____

3. I learned from a storm in my life when _____
_____
_____
_____

4. This passage encourages a positive attitude in the midst of a storm by _____
_____
_____
_____

Learning Station 2

"Saying Goodbye"

Life is full of changes. People change, move away, die, get divorced, become ill or choose a different lifestyle. Worrying about what used to be or could have been is not only anxiety-producing but also a waste of time.

You can't change the past. You can only accept it and go on with your life. You need to let go of those things that used to be but aren't anymore. A peaceful person has learned to accept life's changes with an attitude of hope and perhaps even joyfulness.

Read Philippians 4:4-9 and Matthew 6:25-27. As a group, rewrite Matthew 6:25-27 in your own words. Revise these verses so they talk about accepting the changes in your life and saying goodbye to things that can no longer be the way you want them to be. You might say: "Don't worry that your classes are harder. God has given you the strength to grow and learn."

List changes you've experienced during the last year. Check those changes you've accepted. Circle those that still trouble you. Think about ways you can use your faith to say goodbye to those changes you've had trouble accepting.

Learning Station 3

"On Wings Like Eagles"

Read Isaiah 40:30-31 together as a group.

Peace in the storm is almost impossible without faith. Many people will tell you about storms they never could have survived without faith. Think of storms you've experienced in your life that you were able to weather because of your faith.

Faith is a gift of God that we can nurture. Think of something you do now or something you can do to strengthen your faith. Make a crossword puzzle of your name and the word or phrase you are thinking of. Your name and the word or phrase will need at least one common letter so they can intersect. Notice the examples below.

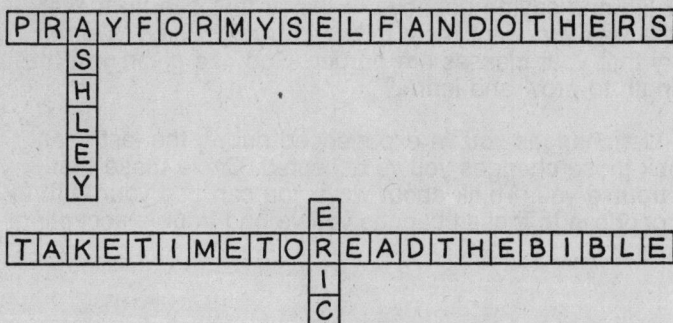

```
P R A Y F O R M Y S E L F A N D O T H E R S
  S
  H
  L
  E
  Y
```

```
                      E
T A K E T I M E T O R E A D T H E B I B L E
                      I
                      C
```

Write your puzzle on the newsprint taped to the wall.

If others have written something you do or would like to do, add your name to their puzzle as well. Some puzzles may end up looking like this:

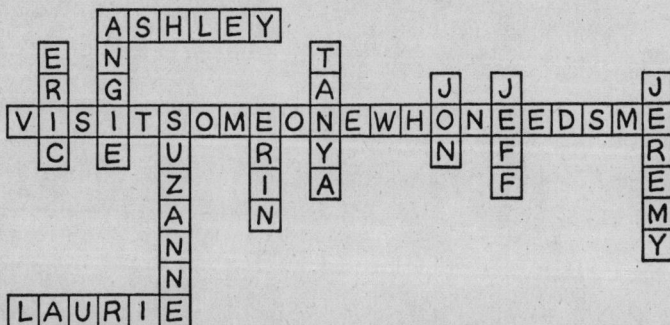

```
      A S H L E Y
  E   N           T
  R   G           A           J   J               J
V I S I T S O M E O N E W H O N E E D S M E
  C   E   U       R   Y   N   F               R
          Z       R   A       F               E
          A       I                           M
          N       N                           Y
          N
L A U R I E
```

Learning Station 4

"What Can We Say?"

If you're like most people, you probably talk to yourself at times. You may hear yourself say: "I can't believe I did something that stupid!" "I'll never pass this test." "I really did it this time!" These negative statements put you down without your even thinking about it.

This kind of "talking to yourself" is called "self-talk," or inner dialogue. Negative self-talk usually outweighs positive self-talk by a tremendous margin. Rarely do you say, "Hey, that was great! You did a good job!" and pat yourself on the back. Negative self-talk can be devastating because it batters your self-esteem, gives you a negative outlook on life and makes it difficult to face life with a hopeful attitude. There's no reason for you to beat yourself with negative self-talk. You are God's and nothing can separate you from him.

Read Romans 8:28-39 with your group. Think of positive self-talk you can use to replace your negative self-talk. Write some positive statements on the newsprint provided. Here are some examples of self-talk.

Negative   **Positive**

1. I'll never pass this test.

This test will be difficult, but I think I can do okay if I study hard.

2. What a stupid thing to do! I bet everybody thinks I'm a stupid jerk.

I'm really embarrassed about what I did. I guess I'll just have to put up with some teasing for a while.

3. I can't do this. I don't even know why I'm trying.

Here's a chance for me to learn something new. I'll probably make some mistakes, but it'll be an interesting challenge.

My Peace in the Storm

Instructions: Looking back at the four learning stations, think about what you have learned. Complete the chart and choose two changes you would like to work on during the coming week. Choose a partner and share your thoughts. Commit to supporting each other as you struggle to change.

Things I do that prevent my having peace or a hopeful attitude:	Things I do that help me feel peaceful:	Changes I would like to make:	How God helps me gain peace:

Amazing Grace

Instructions: Work with your small group to write another verse to "Amazing Grace." It should express what peace in the storm means to you. Write your verse on the newsprint provided. Follow your leader's directions to close this session.

Amazing grace! How sweet the sound,
That saved a wretch like me!
I once was lost, but now am found,
Was blind, but now I see.

Section Two:
Specific Fears and Worries

No One Seems to Care About Me

O ne of the greatest fears people experience is the fear of rejection. This fear keeps individuals from reaching out and making themselves known to others. It keeps them from trying out for the team, applying for a new job or expressing their views in a group. They assume they'll be rejected even before they try. They feel it's not worth risking that awful, sinking, worthless feeling they have when they have been rejected. And yet, is that really true? It's impossible to ask someone for a date, make new friends, get a part in the play or do many of the things that make life meaningful without risking rejection.

Objectives

In this session you will:
- play a game in which you experience rejection.
- rank the areas in which you fear rejection the most.
- discuss your personal experiences with rejection.
- use a problem-solving method to think of ways to minimize or deal with rejection.
- remind each other of the good news that Christ always accepts us.

Rejection Roles

Instructions: Complete the following open-ended statements and talk about your answers within your small group.

1. My role in my group was

2. During the discussion, I felt

5. I liked or disliked this activity because

3. When I contributed to the discussion, other group members

4. I responded to the way the rest of the group treated me by

Rejection Ratings

Instructions: Although most people fear rejection in general, there are situations in which you're more frightened of being rejected than others. Look at the following list and rank each situation in order of how fearful you find the possibility of rejection. Number 1 would be the most fearful and number 12 would be the least fearful.

1   2   3   4   5   6   7   8   9   10   11   12

_____ Trying out for cheerleading or a sports team.

_____ Sharing an idea with my parents.

_____ Volunteering an answer in class.

_____ Asking someone for a date.

_____ Giving a party for a large group from school.

_____ Running for class officer.

_____ Asking a stranger who looks distressed if he needs help.

_____ Saying "Hi" to someone I don't know.

_____ Asking an adult for help with a personal problem.

_____ Sharing a personal fear or weakness with a friend.

_____ Giving someone in youth group a hug.

_____ Telling someone about my faith.

From Rejection to Acceptance

Instructions: Read Romans 5:1-11 and Ephesians 1:3-8. Complete and discuss the following open-ended statements with your partner.

1. I think the most important word in these passages is

2. When I read these passages, I know that Christ

3. The message in these passages makes me feel

Don't Leave Me by Myself

L oneliness is one of the foremost problems facing people today. People of all ages are distant with one another. The suicide rate, especially that of teenagers, keeps climbing. Our society is experiencing more anger and violence than ever before. Finding someone we can trust with our deepest feelings is becoming more and more difficult. Even when we're with a group of friends or our families, we find we're deeply lonely, not because there's no one around but because we don't know how to find someone with whom we can share ourselves. Even when we do find someone who listens and cares about us, we don't know how to open up.

Objectives

In this session you will:

• think about the walls people build that lead to loneliness.

• listen to a psalm of loneliness.

• write a psalm of loneliness.

• discover ways to tear down walls of loneliness.

• practice tearing down loneliness walls by sharing yourself and affirming others.

Something a close friend
should know about me is

When I am feeling
really lonely, I

When I try to tell someone
he or she is important to
me, I feel

Being vulnerable
is scary to me because

Something I would like to do
differently to deal with
loneliness is

What If Someone Tries to Hurt Me?

Today's young people live in a violent world. In the United States, almost 20 percent of teenagers are victims of crime each year. Of those victims, 54 percent know their assailants. Many teenagers imagine that the people who are most likely to hurt them are strangers—the crazed rapist, the desperate drug addict, the serial killer—when, in fact, they are more likely to be raped, abused or hurt by someone they know. Because teenagers don't believe a person close to them would hurt them, they usually aren't prepared to deal with an abusive situation when it arises. What's worse is that after it happens, many teenagers along with their families and friends are likely to blame themselves for what happened and for not doing something to stop it.

Objectives

In this session you will:
• share some of your fears about being hurt or abused by someone you know.
• discover new definitions of abuse and exploitation.
• explore ways to avoid and cope with being hurt or exploited by someone you know.

- focus on ways to support and help others who have been hurt or abused.
- affirm people's worth and value as God's children.
- become familiar with situations that are potentially abusive or exploitative.

Could This Happen to Me?

Instructions: Read the following stories and answer the questions. Be prepared to discuss your answers with a partner.

Tina

Tina was a popular girl at school. She had lots of friends and was active in several clubs and organizations. Tina dated, but she chose not to have sexual intercourse. She felt that waiting for marriage, or at least until she knew she was in love, was the best decision for her.

Tina had been dating Brett for four months, and she really liked him. He was on the football team and active in student government. She felt lucky to be dating him but struggled with his continual pressure to have sex. Sometimes he came over after school while her parents were still at work. They would sit on the couch, kissing and touching each other. Brett wanted to go further, but Tina always managed to persuade him to stop. Even though she was afraid of losing him, Tina made it clear to Brett that she liked him, that she liked kissing and touching him, but she wasn't ready for sexual intercourse.

One spring day when school got out early, Tina and Brett went to her house to study and watch television. As often happened when they were alone without fear of interruption, they ended up on the couch. This time, however, Brett wouldn't take no for an answer. When Tina begged him to stop, he held her down and raped her. Through angry tears, Tina asked him to leave, and he did.

The next day, Tina felt terrible. She had been raped, but she didn't dare tell her parents or some other adult because she wasn't supposed to have boys in the house when her parents weren't there. When she confided her pain and hurt to her best friend, the friend said Tina could only blame herself for leading Brett on. Feeling good about finally scoring with Tina, Brett asked if he could see her again after school.

1. Was Tina right to feel hurt and angry about what had happened? Why or why not?

2. Was Brett right to do what he did? Why or why not?

3. Is it ever okay to force another person to have sexual intercourse? Why or why not? If your answer is yes, under what circumstances is it okay?

4. Have you known someone who's been raped by a date or a friend? Be prepared to talk about the experience, without revealing who the person is.

5. Have you ever been afraid or cautious because you were afraid someone you knew might rape you? Explain.

6. Have you ever felt pressured to go further sexually than you wanted? Explain.

7. Do you think something like this could happen to you or someone you know? Why or why not?

continued

Chris

Chris was smaller than most other boys in the 10th-grade. He wasn't athletic, but he did well in other areas such as writing, computers, science and music. Some students teased him about his size, but most of the time Chris felt okay about himself. He had some good friends, and they did things together during and after school. He even had a few girls interested in him. Most of the time, he was happy with school and his life.

In the middle of the year, however, some tough boys decided to pick on Chris. At first they just teased him, called him names and said cruel things about his lack of size and athletic ability. Chris would respond with funny comments or completely ignore them. Later the boys started to get physical. They would "accidentally" bump into him in the halls or shove him when he walked by. Chris told them to stop it and leave him alone, but they just laughed.

Soon he noticed that some of the boys would stand and stare at him as he ate his lunch or talked to his friends. He began to feel nervous and hesitated to go anywhere alone at school. When he found a threatening note in his locker, he shared his dilemma with his favorite teacher, who reported it to the assistant principal. The boys were called into the office for a conference. Later that day, one of the boys who had been harassing Chris threw him up against a locker and told him they were going to make school even more miserable for him. He informed Chris that he hadn't seen anything yet! Afraid to go to school the next day, Chris pretended he was sick.

1. Was Chris right to be afraid? Why or why not?

2. Was he right to handle the situation the way he did? Why or why not? What would you have done?

3. Have you ever known anyone who experienced violence at school? Talk about it with your partner.

4. Have you ever been concerned about your personal safety at school? Explain.

What Does the Bible Say About . . . ?

Instructions: Read your assigned passage and answer the questions that follow it. (See the examples.) Discuss your answers within your small group. Add other questions or concerns that come out of your discussion.

Psalm 8

What does this passage say about...
- the value God gives all people? *He has made people a little lower than the heavenly beings and has crowned them with glory and honor.*

- a person using others for gain or selfish pleasure? *God is concerned about all people he has created, including the victims.*

- what you should do if someone you know is being exploited? *Use the power God gave me to take care of his creation, including humans.*

- how you should feel about yourself? *To be created a little less than heavenly beings says I am valuable.*

- other questions and concerns? *What does it mean to silence the foe and the avenger? How am I responsible for that?*

Matthew 10:28-31

What does this passage say about . . .
- your value in God's eyes? _____

_____

- your worries about being sexually or physically abused? _____

_____

- your right to say no to someone when you have placed yourself in a difficult situation? _____

_____

- a person blaming and disliking herself after she has been sexually abused or raped? _____

_____

- other questions and concerns? _____

_____

continued

Luke 6:27-36

What does this passage say about . . .
- respecting another person's wishes? _____
_____

- getting help for a sexual abuser? _____
_____

- forcing another person to do something against his or her will? ___
_____
_____

- how you should expect others to treat you? _____
_____
_____

- other questions and concerns? _____

Luke 10:25-28

What does this passage say about . . .
- a boy raping his date because she's had sex with other guys and he thought it wouldn't matter? _____
_____

- a group of boys tricking a girl into coming to a party and trying to sexually assault her? _____
_____

- reporting someone who repeatedly harasses teenagers in school or at work? _____
_____

- taking advantage of someone who is smaller or weaker? _____
_____
_____

- other questions and concerns? _____
_____
_____

continued

1 Corinthians 13:1-7

What does this passage say about . . .
• trying to persuade your date to do something you know he or she doesn't want to do? _____

_____

• a teenager trying to get help for his or her alcoholic, physically abusive family?_____

_____

• responding to a friend who was raped while drunk? _____

_____

_____

• how to feel when a bully gets badly beaten up? _____

_____

_____

• other questions and concerns? _____

_____

Ephesians 4:31-32

What does this passage say about . . .
• dealing with those people who make you angry? _____

_____

_____

• how you should expect people who love you to treat you?____

_____

_____

• your response to sexual abuse or harassment?_____

_____

_____

• using a person to explore and enjoy sex with? _____

_____

• other questions and concerns? _____

continued

_____

Colossians 3:12-17

What does this passage say about . . .
• deciding how to respond to someone who has wronged you? _____

_____

_____

_____

• a girl saying no to sex even though she said some things that made her boyfriend think she was going to say yes? _____

_____

_____

_____

• your response to a person who's recovering from physical or sexual abuse in his or her family?_____

_____

_____

_____

• your fears about being hurt by someone you know? _____

_____

_____

• other questions and concerns? _____

_____

_____

Even If / Even When / Because

Instructions: List four to six ways to complete the open-ended statement assigned to you and your partner. Base your list on the things you and the groups have talked about during this meeting. Here are two examples:

Statement: You have the right to say no to sex even . . .

Completions: *if your date thinks your clothes are sexy.*

if you thought you wanted to say yes.

if you are out with someone your parents said
you can't date.

if your date spent a lot of money on you.

Statement: You are a child of God, loved and chosen by him, even . . .

Completions: *when you make a mistake*

when you feel abused and misused.

when other people make you feel like an object to be
used and misused.

when others tell you that you're no good.

Statements for you to try:
  You can say no to sexual harassment because . . .
  You have value in God's eyes even . . .
  You can expect your friends to support you even . . .
  You can do something about sexual abuse even . . .
  You have the right to say no to sex even . . .
  You can show love to friends and family even . . .
  You have the right to expect not to be physically abused because . . .
  You can expect your date to respect your wishes because . . .
  You can ask the people who care about you for help even . . .

Statement: _____

Completions: _____

  _____

  _____

  _____

What If I Fail?

"I really messed that up!" "I could *never* do that." "I can't do anything right!" Christians often say these things because they're afraid of failing or not measuring up. Many teenagers are afraid of failure. They live in a world where they're constantly evaluated by school, friends, parents and employers.

School can be an especially fearful place for people who worry about failing. Pressures to have good grades, hang around with the right friends, make the team, get a leading role, be in the right clubs and get into first-choice colleges are enormous. It's no wonder that some choose to withdraw into drugs or drinking, depression, isolation or even suicide.

Many teenagers equate failing with being a failure. These same young people are often so afraid of failure that they refuse to try and never discover their true abilities.

Objectives
In this session you will:
• evaluate the way you cope with your fear of failure.
• think about how your friends cope with fear of failure.
• discuss your strongest fears about failing.

- read and discuss a story about success and failure.
- look at Peter as an example of both success and failure.
- offer advice to one another on how to deal with the fears of failure.
- learn that failing isn't the same as being a failure.
- discover how your friends see you as "dressed for success."

How Am I Doing?

Instructions: Use the following quiz to evaluate how you deal with failure. Read the two choices in each situation and circle the one that best describes the behavior you would choose.

I'm more likely to . . .

study hard and do my best on a test.	or	study, but cheat on a test to make sure I do as well as possible.
plan and do an important school project carefully, allowing myself plenty of time to complete it.	or	worry and procrastinate about an important school project, start it late and then complain the completed project would have been better if I had had more time.
try out for the newly formed debate team at school, even if I'm not sure I can learn to debate.	or	decide not to try out for the debate team even though it sounds fun. I don't want to make a fool of myself by messing up.
work hard on a dance or gymnastics routine, then relax and enjoy myself during the competition.	or	work hard on a dance or gymnastics routine, but feel so nervous about the competition that I don't perform well.
after failing the first chemistry test of the year, meet with the teacher to discover what I can do to improve.	or	after failing the first chemistry test of the year, decide chemistry isn't my subject and resign myself to poor chemistry grades for the rest of the year.
after losing a school election, congratulate the winner and offer my help and support in upcoming projects.	or	after losing a school election, stay out of student government altogether and make snide comments about the election and the winners.

continued

after hearing my parents' 1000th lecture on my poor grades in school and their 2000th comparison with my straight-A sister, think of the things I do well. Realize I have some talents such as athletics, helping at home, music, work and making friends in addition to things I need to improve.

or

after hearing my parents' 1000th lecture on my poor grades in school and their 2000th comparison with my straight-A sister, decide that I'm really a failure. Realize that if something doesn't happen soon, I'll be a failure all my life.

before an audition, imagine that the experience will be fun, interesting and challenging. I'll look forward to it.

or

before an audition, worry and imagine everything that could go wrong. I'll picture myself as I would feel if I failed miserably.

seek help from a counselor when I'm unhappy and try to take responsibility for my own happiness.

or

blame my unhappiness on anything or anyone available and continue being unhappy while refusing to admit I need help.

after discovering an optional extra-credit project is much harder than I expected, get serious and do whatever it takes to succeed.

or

after discovering an optional extra-credit project is much harder than I expected, decide that I don't need the extra credit and tell the teacher I changed my mind.

Total _____   Total _____

Total the number of choices in the two columns. If most of your answers are in the left-hand column, you handle your fear of failure well. It doesn't control your life, keep you from doing the things you want to do or keep you in a constant state of depression about being a failure. If most of your answers are in the right-hand column, you're probably struggling with your fear of failure. You have trouble seeing failure as a learning experience and separating failing from being a failure. If your answers are evenly divided or close on both sides you probably have specific areas where you have trouble coping with your fear of failure.

What a Nightmare!

Instructions: Read the story and follow the directions for the activities that follow. Discuss your responses with your partner and the large group.

"What a nightmare," said Debi Thomas after her disappointing performance in women's figure skating at the 1988 Winter Olympics. Taking a year off from medical school, Debi had spent endless hours training and practicing for this special event. But she left her hopes for the gold medal on the ice after she faltered on several important jumps. The artistic Katarina Witt of East Germany won the gold, and the silver went to Canada's Elizabeth Manley, who moved from third to second in front of her home crowd. Debi received the bronze, which was one of only six medals won by the United States in these Olympics.

The crowd and judges had expected a duel between Debi and Katarina from the start. Katarina won the gold in 1984 and had been beaten only once since then, by Debi in the 1986 world championships. Going into the finals, the competition turned out as expected, with Debi holding a slight lead. If either skater made a mistake, the other was sure to win. Katarina skated beautifully but conservatively, counting on her acting and artistic form to increase her score. Debi, the more athletic skater, moved powerfully into her first jump combination, but landed awkwardly. Shaken by her error, she faltered on two other jumps and the gold slipped away.

These are some of Debi's comments following her performance:

"It wasn't my night. I knew it would be a long wait [she skated last] and I knew it would be hard. I tried to put everything in it, but I guess now I can go back to school."

"It was hard to stay 'psyched up' for the whole thing, but I'm not going to make any excuses . . . It wasn't supposed to happen, I guess. But I tried."

"The whole reason for being here was to skate great, and after missing it I couldn't skate great . . . It was hard for me to keep going."

"I'm not that devastated. I thought it would be a lot worse. I thought I would cry and throw things."

When asked if she would work toward the 1992 Olympics, she responded, "No way."

Complete the following statements:
1. A time I felt I had failed at something important was

_____

_____

continued

2. A time I performed poorly because I was worried about not doing well was_____

_____

3. Debi Thomas should see herself as a success/failure (choose one) because _____.

_____

4. Debi did/did not (choose one) handle her loss of the gold medal well because_____

_____

5. If I had been Debi, I think I would have _____

_____

Check all statements that apply:
6. I think Debi lost the gold because . . .

_____ Too much pressure was put on her by the media and all the talk about a duel between her and Katarina.

_____ She had to skate last and had too much time to worry before her performance.

_____ After making one mistake, she didn't want to continue an imperfect performance.

_____ She got "psyched out" by the knowledge that Katarina was extremely difficult to beat.

_____ She lost her nerve after making her first mistake.

7. List things that point to Debi's being a winner in spite of her losing the gold medal. _____

_____

_____

8. When you're struggling, how do you remind yourself that you're not a failure? _____

I'M OK

_____

_____

Dressed for Success

Instructions: List those things that make you a success in God's eyes. Sign your name at the bottom of the page and pass your book around so others can list other things they see that makes you successful in God's eyes.

"Therefore, as God's chosen people, holy and dearly loved, clothe yourselves with compassion, kindness, humility, gentleness and patience. Bear with each other and forgive whatever grievances you may have against one another. Forgive as the Lord forgave you. And over all these virtues put on love, which binds them all together in perfect unity.

"Let the peace of Christ rule in your hearts, since as members of one body you were called to peace. And be thankful. Let the word of Christ dwell in you richly as you teach and admonish one another with all wisdom, and as you sing psalms, hymns and spiritual songs with gratitude in your hearts to God. And whatever you do, whether in word or deed, do it all in the name of the Lord Jesus, giving thanks to God the Father through him" (Colossians 3:12-17).

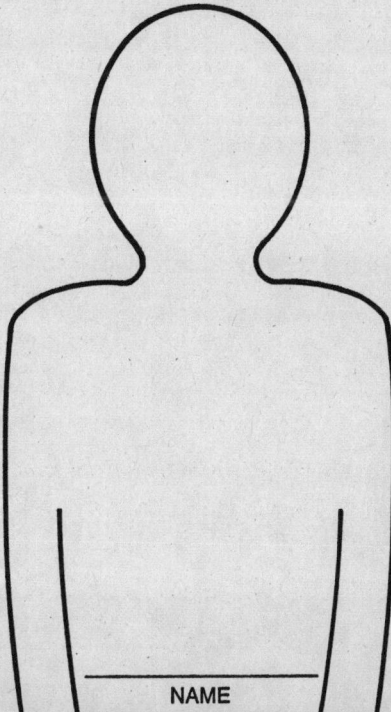

NAME

■ SESSION NINE
What Am I Going to Do With My Life?

This question becomes more of a struggle as teenagers progress through their high school years. During the senior year, it becomes a constant worry for many young people. Some kids choose their career and get started on their educational path easily. Others get confused with their endless choices, but eventually move toward a goal that interests them. For the few who have no idea what they want to do with their lives, choosing a path for the future seems almost impossible and extremely frightening.

Fear of the future is normal, and worrying about choosing a career isn't unusual. Seniors in high school rarely know what they want to do with the rest of their life.

Objectives
In this session you will:
• share a career choice you're considering at this time.
• learn about Moses' fears when God called him to a new career.
• discuss your fears as you plan your future.
• explore some things about yourself that will affect your career choices.
• utilize two methods to explore career possibilities.
• set specific career-search goals.

Who, Me?

Instructions: With your partner, read Exodus 3:1—4:17. Answer the questions and discuss your responses.

1. Moses seriously doubted his ability to be a leader. What are some of your self-doubts as you prepare for your future?

2. Moses had a handicap he thought would prevent him from answering God's call. (He stuttered.) What holds you back when you think of preparing for a career?

3. Moses was deathly afraid of the task God called him to do. What are you afraid of when you think of preparing for a particular occupation?

4. Moses gave God excuses for why he couldn't do what God commanded. How do you avoid dealing with the fearful parts of preparing for a career?

5. God called Moses because God knew that with his help, Moses could do the job. In what ways does God help you in your career choice and preparation?

What Kind of Animal Are You?

Instructions: Read the category and description for the animal you chose most often. If you chose several different animals, read each description you chose. Discuss with your partner how the descriptions fit or don't fit.

1. Crafty Cobra. People who choose this category often prefer working with tools and objects instead of people and words. This type of person might also like working with plants and/or animals. Jobs that might interest a person in this category include dental technician, electrician, park ranger, auto mechanic, airline pilot, carpenter and groundskeeper.

2. Conventional Cheetah. People who choose this category probably prefer well-defined duties that require systematic organizational skills. These people enjoy working with data, have an ability to work with numbers and usually place a high value on status and financial success. Occupations that fall into this category include accountant, secretary, computer operator, ticket agent, bookkeeper and various bank occupations.

3. Enterprising Emu. People who choose this category are usually skilled with words, enjoy leading others and find it easy to persuade others, either to see things their way or to buy something. Careers in this category include management, sales, law and detective work.

continued

4. Intellectual Impala. People who choose this category enjoy working alone. They value scientific and mathematical work. Some of their characteristics include curiosity, creativity, studiousness and observational skills. Careers in this category include engineering, architecture, medicine, computer programming and science.

5. Artistic Antelope. People who choose this category are interested in careers that use their creative abilities and allow them to express themselves. These individuals usually prefer a non-conforming lifestyle and an unstructured work situation. They also place great value on independence. Careers in this category include art, music, writing and entertainment.

6. Helpful Hyena. People who choose this category like to work with other people in a helping role. They get along well with others and are concerned for others' well-being. Careers in this category include counseling, teaching, nursing and social work.

Did you find yourself? Great! But if none of the career ideas on these pages appealed to you, don't be discouraged. This is an abbreviated interest survey as well as an abbreviated list of careers. Check in your school guidance office or your local library for more detailed interest inventories and career guides. An excellent help in finding career information is the *Guide for Occupational Exploration* (U.S. Government Printing Office) available in most libraries.

In Search of a Career

Instructions: Think carefully about the following open-ended statements and complete them. Be as honest with yourself as possible.

1. When I'm free to do what I want, the activities I enjoy most are _Softball, music, video games_

2. I think of myself as _growing closer to God in ensurce more self esteem_

3. For me, the most important thing about a career is _happiness_

4. The school subjects I find most interesting are _Computer learning_

5. A volunteer activity that has meant a lot to me is _City teams_

6. An extracurricular activity I've enjoyed or been interested in is _Softball_

7. The level of education I hope to attain is _Ordained Ministre_

8. A few things I'm good at include _towing, softball, video games_

9. Ten years from now, I would like to be _full time in ministry of some sort_

Examine your responses to these statements for clues in your search for a career.

For more activities and information to help you discover where your career interests lie, borrow or buy a copy of Richard N. Bolles' *What Color Is Your Parachute?* (Ten Speed Press). It contains helpful information about job hunting and can help you identify what you're looking for.

How Do I Look?

It's no wonder looks rate high on teenagers' list of worries. Many TV and movie stars have perfect faces and figures. Advertisements continually bombard the public telling people how to lose more weight, have a brighter smile, grow healthy nails or get rid of pimples. Fitness centers assure individuals, "You owe it to yourself to get in shape." In addition to the media blitz, young people begin to see the obvious—attractive people seem to get more dates, have more friends, make higher salaries and just get more of the "good" things in life.

In his book *Hide or Seek* (Revell), James Dobson calls beauty a "gold coin" that opens many doors and makes life easier for the lucky few who are blessed with good looks. As Dobson points out, however, physical beauty is the exception rather than the rule. Most people are average looking, with good and bad points.

Society teaches people from an early age to work hard to look their best. Many individuals focus so much on the problems with their looks that they forget to look at their other good points—a compassionate heart, a lively sense of humor or a creative mind. Many quite attractive people never see their beauty because they are worrying about every physical flaw, real or imagined. As many as 10 to 15 percent of young women and 4 to 7 percent of young men suffer from eating disorders. Their mental image of their body is so distorted that they diet or purge incessantly to keep losing or to keep from gaining weight. Some of these people develop serious health problems; some even die.

Objectives

In this session you will:

- discuss your concerns about how you look.
- rate the importance of physical and other characteristics for yourself, a friend, the media and God.
- compare what the media say is important with what God says is important.
- discover positive ways to deal with problems with one's looks.
- affirm that each person is created in God's image.

In Media's Eyes / In God's Eyes

Instructions: Title one sheet of newsprint "In Media's Eyes." Using the magazines your leader gave you, work with your group to make a list of the characteristics the media think you should have.

Title the other sheet of newsprint "In God's Eyes." Using the following Bible passages, work with your group to make a list of the characteristics God wants you to have.

Matthew 18:21-35	James 2:1-13
Luke 6:46-49	1 Peter 5:5-7
Philippians 3:20—4:1	2 Peter 1:3-11
Colossians 3:15-17	1 John 3:11
2 Thessalonians 3:6-15	3 John 1:11

When you've finished your lists, create two brief commercials for your group to present to the others. One commercial should be from the media ("Make sure your breath is clean!"); the other should be from God ("Make sure you do what is good."). Try to get as many items as possible from your lists into your respective commercials. Be creative and have fun.

In Media's Eyes

In God's Eyes

What's It Worth to Me?

Instructions: Read the following statements. Mark where you stand on each continuum of what that statement is worth to you.

1. I'd miss a party if I had a big, ugly pimple on my nose.
It's worth it! --No way!

2. I'd diet until I was physically sick in order to be happy with my weight.
It's worth it! --No way!

3. I'd use steroids to build up my body even though I know that they can cause serious, long-term health problems.
It's worth it! --No way!

4. I'd get up an hour earlier than necessary in order to make sure my hair, makeup and clothes were perfect.
It's worth it! --No way!

5. I'd avoid the person I have a huge crush on if I'd just finished gym class and hadn't been able to take a shower or comb my hair.
It's worth it! --No way!

6. I'd expect people not to like me if I didn't wear the right clothes or look perfect.
It's worth it! --No way!

7. I'd work out every day to get my body in good shape.
It's worth it! --No way!

8. I'd choose clothes carefully, being aware of what colors and styles flatter me most.
It's worth it! --No way!

9. I'd eat a healthy diet and avoid junk food.
It's worth it! --No way!

10. I'd have plastic surgery to change something about my face or body that I was unhappy with.
It's worth it! --No way!

11. When I don't look my best, I'm likely to worry about it so much that I don't have a good time.
It's worth it! --No way!

12. I'm more likely to worry about my looks than my friendships.
It's worth it! --No way!

13. I'm more likely to spend time worrying about my looks than about my relationship with God.
It's worth it! --No way!

Look at where you placed yourself in each situation. Are there things you'd like to change? Which attitudes about the importance of your looks seem unhealthy? Circle one or two areas you'd like to work on.

What If It All Blows Up?

Nuclear war. The apocalypse. Will it happen in this generation? Many teenagers seem to think so. In a recent study, more than a third of a group of high school students agreed that nuclear annihilation would be the fate of all humanity in their lifetime. But other studies report that school, looks, sex, drugs and peer relationships rate higher on the worry scale for young people than the threat of nuclear war.

What is the significance of these two extremes? For one thing, the studies indicate that some teenagers *are* worried about the nuclear threat. Some are honestly afraid of the possibility that life as they know it will end soon. Most teenagers are aware of the possibility of nuclear war, but how does that awareness affect the way they live? Could this be the reason so many young people seem to be "living for today"? Is this why kids don't seem concerned about their future? Maybe. It's important to help these young people understand and remember God's promises. He has told us that we are his children and he is with us until the end of time—even in a nuclear nightmare.

Objectives

In this session you will:

• play a simulation game about surviving a

nuclear war.

• share your opinion about issues related to nuclear war.

• discuss your fears about nuclear war.

• use God's promises to respond to your worries about nuclear war.

• discover your responsibility in preventing nuclear war.

• affirm your faith in God's promises in the shadow of nuclear war.

BALLOT

Instructions: Put a checkmark by the skills you will need in your post-nuclear society. Remember you can select only half of the group.

☐ Business executive

☐ Medical doctor and professor

☐ Politician

☐ Psychologist

☐ Social worker

☐ Priest

☐ Homemaker

☐ Nurse

☐ _____

☐ _____

☐ _____

☐ Building contractor

☐ Farmer

☐ Mechanic

☐ Day laborer

☐ Water treatment specialist

☐ Computer programmer

☐ Dentist

☐ _____

☐ _____

☐ _____

Bad News/GOOD NEWS

Instructions: Read the statement assigned to you, the bad news and then the good news. Work with your small group to prepare a "bad news" report. (Read a "bad news" statement adding facts and figures that support the idea.) Then prepare a "good news" report based on the Bible verse. Don't just read the Bible verse. Explain how it tells us to live, hope or believe in a time of nuclear threat. (For example, God reminds you to live life fully because he's in control.) Share your reports with the other groups.

1. Bad news—Every city in America with a population of 25,000 or more people is a target for a nuclear device.

Good news—Lamentations 3:21-24

2. Bad news—The people living at ground zero in a nuclear attack would die instantly; those living farther away would die more slowly from fallout and radiation.

Good news—Colossians 1:21-23, 27

3. Bad news—People hiding in shelters during a nuclear attack would likely die despite their protection because of fire and heat, oxygen depletion or the concussion of the blast.

Good news—Hebrews 6:13-20

4. Bad news—Survivors of a nuclear war would face a world without life-support systems or medical assistance. There would be no immunity to new diseases.

Good news—John 6:35-40

5. Bad news—A ballistic missile takes less than 30 minutes to travel from the United States to the Soviet Union, or vice versa, meaning that little time is available for reaching safety, if there is any.

Good news—John 11:25-26

"Bad news" facts are from David Augsburger, *When Enough Is Enough* (Ventura, CA: Regal Books, 1984), 161-162 and Richard L. Zweigenhaft, "Students Surveyed About Nuclear War," Bulletin of the Atomic Scientists. (February 1985), 26.

74

What Can I Do?

Instructions: Listen to the story, then answer the questions. Be prepared to share your answers with the group.

1. When I think of doing something about nuclear war, I
_____
_____

2. The best way to prevent nuclear war is _____
_____
_____

3. I can help prevent nuclear war by _____
_____
_____

4. I can work for peace in my daily life by _____
_____
_____

5. I plan to start by _____
_____
_____

What's Going to Happen to Me?

One of the greatest fears children have is the fear of abandonment. The "separation anxiety" expressed by infants or toddlers when parents leave them with a babysitter is an example of that fear. Children aren't sure their mom and dad will come back. As children get older, they learn that parents do come back. In this way children begin to trust their mom and dad to be there whenever they need them.

Teenagers aren't little children, but they still worry about losing a parent. As they move toward independence, young people still need some security in difficult times, not to mention financial support. Loss of or separation from a parent during the teenage years can be traumatic.

Young people worry, "What's going to happen to me?" Financial plans for things such as music lessons or college tuition may be altered. Emotional support may be lacking from the surviving or custodial parent because of the personal struggles he or she is facing alone. Teenagers may be pushed into maturity too fast, or they may regress to more immature behavior. Decisions made now can affect these young people for the rest of their lives.

Objectives

In this session you will:

• share a time you experienced a loss that affected you deeply.

• discuss the fears you have related to parents getting a divorce or a parent dying.

• learn about the stages of grief a person usually experiences after a loss.

• hear about people's actual experiences with the death or divorce of parents.

• discover the skills you have and those you can develop to help you cope with a loss.

• affirm the strength you receive from God when you're suffering.

Stages of Grief

Instructions: Read the following to clarify your understanding of how grief operates in both death and divorce. Think about how these stages fit an important loss you (or a friend) may have experienced. In the space that follows, list the evidence of each stage in your own (or your friend's) experience.

When a person experiences the loss of someone (such as a parent) or something important to him or her (such as the parents' marriage), the person usually goes through a period of grieving. Grief is a natural reaction to loss. It's unreasonable not to expect to grieve over the loss of someone or something important in your life. The process of grieving typically happens in several stages.

continued

Stage one. Usually, this is the stage of shock or disbelief. The person may deny that the divorce is happening or even that the death occurred. This reaction isn't unusual and can be a healthy way to allow time for the person to adjust to the pain of this loss. It's important for the person who has experienced loss to have the opportunity to express his or her feelings and to have people who will listen. With death, the funeral is an important part of the grieving process because it offers family and friends a socially acceptable setting in which to grieve.

Stage two. During this stage the person has accepted the loss and is struggling to adjust to it. This period contains frequent ups and downs as the person bounces back and forth between shock and recovery. Feelings he or she might experience include loneliness, sadness, depression, anger, hurt and possibly guilt. The person might feel guilty about things that were said or not said. The individual might be angry at one or both parents for letting the divorce happen, sad that the family is no longer intact or depressed about a seeming loss of control over his or her life. Friends or significant adults who will listen with care are important during this time.

Stage three. This final stage of the grief process is the recovery stage. It may take six months for some people to reach this stage or two years for others. Although the person still experiences periods of loneliness or sadness, the loss is no longer the central focus of his or her life.

(These stages are general descriptions and shouldn't be considered standards for every grief experience. There can be quite a few variations, depending on the individual situation.)

Evidences of grief

Stage one: Stage two: Stage three:

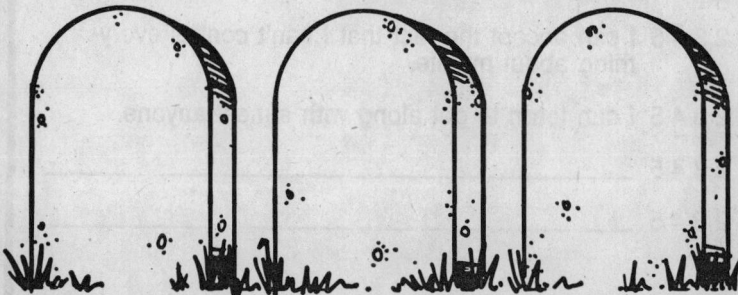

How Well Do I Cope?

Instructions: Rate your coping skills by circling a number by each statement.

  1=I don't manage that particular skill well.
  3=I have average ability in that skill.
  5=That skill is one of my best.

  At the end of the list add one or two skills you have that weren't listed, skills that have helped you cope with loss.

1 2 3 4 5 I'm not afraid to let myself cry.

1 2 3 4 5 I adapt well to new situations.

1 2 3 4 5 I'm willing to seek professional help if I need it.

1 2 3 4 5 I can be assertive in getting my friends to listen to me when I need to talk, even when I need to talk about difficult feelings.

1 2 3 4 5 I can accept my feelings and the feelings of others, both positive and negative.

1 2 3 4 5 I know that when life gets difficult, things will eventually get better.

1 2 3 4 5 I count on my faith to help me get through hard times.

1 2 3 4 5 I choose to express my feelings in nondestructive ways.

1 2 3 4 5 I can go on with my life even though things aren't the way I wish they were.

1 2 3 4 5 I can accept the fact that I can't control everything about my life.

1 2 3 4 5 I can learn to get along with almost anyone.

1 2 3 4 5 _____

1 2 3 4 5 _____

It's Not Safe to Go Outside

Violence has become the #1 cause of teenage death in the United States. The #1 killer of teenagers is automobile accidents, and the #2 killer is homicide. Although in recent years much has been said about crime against senior citizens, crime against teenagers is much more common. Teenagers are four times more likely to be robbed and 17 times more likely to be assaulted than senior citizens. Going outside can seem extremely unsafe to most teenagers.

Objectives

In this session you will:

• tell about a fearful experience you've had with crime.

• share the things that worry you most about crime.

• discuss ways to live faithfully and fearlessly.

• seek specific solutions to potential crime situations.

• look for words of faith and security in the Bible.

Being Faithful, Being Fearful

Instructions: Read Luke 10:25-37. Rewrite the parable of the good Samaritan as it might happen today, with you as the good Samaritan. Don't change the facts or ending; just rewrite the story as if it happened in modern times with you as the hero. For example: "On my way to youth group, I drove past the park. While I sat at the stoplight, I noticed a young boy crying. A young couple walked by, glanced at him and continued their walk. A middle-aged jogger approached him from behind, checked his watch and hurried on . . ."

When you've finished, complete the open-ended statements at the end of the worksheet.

_____
_____
_____
_____
_____
_____
_____
_____
_____
_____
_____
_____

If this actually happened and I did what I just wrote,

1. My parents would say . . . _____
_____

2. My friends would say . . . _____
_____

3. God would say . . . _____
_____

4. I would feel . . . _____
_____

5. In a situation like this, I think I would probably respond by . . . _____
_____

Livin' in the Real World

Instructions: Here are some real-life situations you might face. In fact, some of you may have already dealt with situations like these. Some situations involve asking yourself how to live faithfully as well as safely; others deal with safety alone. Read each situation and list your responses to the open-ended statements.

1. You're home alone and you're nervous. There've been numerous break-ins in your neighborhood. You worry that someone might try to break in while you're at home alone.
   a. Things I could do to feel less fearful are . . .

   b. Things I could ask others to do to help me feel less fearful are . . .

2. You work at a store in the mall. Your job requires you to close at the end of the day, which is usually after 10 p.m. You worry about walking to your car alone. This is especially frightening since there've been several holdups and attempted abductions in the parking lots in your town.
   a. Things I could do to feel less fearful are . . .

   b. Things I could ask others to do to help me feel less fearful are . . .

PARKING

continued

3. You and several friends are attending a movie. A man sitting alone several seats from you seems to be sick, but you're not sure.

a. The safest thing for me to do is . . .

b. I think God would want me to . . .

c. I could help this man and still feel safe by . . .

4. A man in your neighborhood keeps complaining to you that he needs help with work in his yard. You don't know him very well, but something about him makes you feel uneasy. You think he wants you to help him, but you feel more comfortable staying away from him.

a. The safest thing for me to do is . . .

b. I think God would want me to . . .

c. I could help this man and still feel safe by . . .

5. In the parking lot at the shopping center, a man approaches you for help to get his car started. He asks to ride with you as you drive to his car.

a. The safest thing for me to do is . . .

b. I think God would want me to . . .

c. I could help this man and still feel safe by . . .